Unbridled Creativity:

101 Writing Exercises for the Horse Lover

Susan Friedland

Unbridled Creativity:
101 Writing Exercises for the Horse Lover

Cover Design: Amy Summer Ellison
Editor: Holly Caccamise
Photos: Carolyn Rikje and Susan Friedland
ISBN: 978-1-7327105-4-2
Print Edition
Susan Friedland
saddleseekshorse.com

Susan Friedland

UNBRIDLED CREATIVITY:
101 WRITING EXERCISES FOR THE HORSE LOVER

Susan Friedland, an award-winning equestrian blogger at Saddle Seeks Horse, is a middle school teacher by day and horse girl 24/7. Susan's first book ***Horses Adored and Men Endured: a Memoir of Falling and Getting Back Up*** garnered praise from *UnTacked*, *Horse and Style*, and Jean Abernethy, the creator of Fergus the Horse. Susan's follow-up book ***Strands of Hope: How to Grieve the Loss of a Horse*** is a practical guide for the grieving equestrian. Saddle Seeks Horse, the blog, features product reviews, riding inspiration and candid talk about life with horses. Susan's articles about horses and the people who love them have appeared in *Horse Illustrated*, *Young Rider* and *Sidelines*. Connect with Susan at saddleseekshorse.com or on Instagram @saddleseekshorse.

Author's Note About How to Use This Book

Dear Reader and Writer,

I'm excited you're here and eager to write! As much as I love riding horses, I find joy also in writing about them on my blog Saddle Seeks Horse. My guess is you adore horses and writing too, and that's how you found *Unbridled Creativity: 101 Writing Exercises for the Horse Lover*. Pleased to meet you!

With over 20 years of classroom experience as a teacher, I've merged education's best practices for writing instruction with horsey themes for your journaling pleasure.

"Mentor texts" are a powerful way to get students writing. That fancy term means writing models. For example, if someone is confused on how to structure a persuasive essay or pen a limerick, by showing persuasive essays or limericks to the aspiring writer, creativity will ignite and the words will begin to flow. Check out mentor texts for several prompts in this book at saddleseeksshorse.com/horse-writing-prompts for your inspiration.

This book is organized so the prompts generally start out simple and grow in complexity. You don't have to go through them in numerical order. Feel free to skip around. Also, If you want to share your writing on social media, I would love to see it! Tag me on Facebook or Instagram at @saddleseeksshorse.

Lastly, if you are a fan of this book, could you tell a friend who also likes to write? Word-of-mouth recommendation is powerful, as are reviews on Amazon or Good Reads. More reviews and recommendations will increase discoverability of this book for people like us who enjoy both horses and writing. Thank you!

I'm excited you want to hone your writing skills and nurture your creativity with me. Have fun and happy writing!

Susan

Table of Contents

12 Ways to Be a Better Writer

1. Read a ton. All kinds of writing. Read widely.
2. Keep lists of ideas and topics that interest you.
3. Write frequently.
4. Keep a journal.
5. Read your own writing aloud.
6. Befriend other writers.
7. Join a writer's group.
8. Do NaNoWriMo.
9. Start a blog.
10. Work with a writing coach.
11. Take courses on writing, whether in person or online.
12. Find a passion, and express yourself in writing on that theme.

If you are looking for a writing coach, I can help you. Visit saddleseekshorse.com/work-with-me

Lovely Lists

Lists don't get the credit they deserve. Instead of lowly organizational tools scribbled on sticky notes or the back of junk mail envelopes, lists can encourage a loved one ("21 reasons I think you're cool"), motivate you to pursue a goal, or keep you focused during a crazy time. I believe lists are lovely and fun, and you know who else does? Everyone. People LOVE listicles (such a silly word, right?) and respond to them. Some of my most popular blog posts started out as lists:

- 7 Reasons You Should Always Wear a Helmet When You Ride
- 5 Horse Memoirs to Add to Your Reading List
- 42 Best Horse Trailer Shopping Tips.

Now it's your turn to lunge into lists.

Write down all the things a new horse owner would need prior to welcoming his or her new horse home.

_____

_____

_____

_____

_____

_____

_____

_____

_____

_____

_____

Name 10 people you never would have met without horses. Select one and write about how you met and what your relationship means to you.

_____

_____

_____

_____

_____

_____

_____

_____

_____

_____

_____

Brainstorm a list of 10 horse show or racing names you would like to name 10 horses. Go! (Visit saddleseekshorse.com/horse-writing-prompts for the mentor text for prompt #3.)

_____

_____

_____

_____

_____

_____

_____

_____

_____

_____

Make a list of all the horses you've ridden. If there are too many to count, start with last week and work backward three years, or start with your first ride and work forward three years. Next, choose your top three favorite rides and explain why those were so special.

_____

_____

_____

_____

_____

_____

_____

_____

_____

List as many horse movies as you can. Put a star next to your top three. In a paragraph or two, justify why those movies are your top picks.

_____

_____

_____

_____

_____

_____

_____

_____

_____

_____

Record three lessons you've learned the hard way with horses. Elaborate on the lessons. (For an extra challenge, share this information with someone younger than you, so you can potentially spare them from the school of hard knocks.)

_____

_____

_____

_____

_____

_____

_____

_____

List all the things you would see in a typical tack room. Once you have a long list of nouns, pair an adjective with each one.

_____

_____

_____

_____

_____

_____

_____

_____

_____

_____

Itemize all the features you would have if you built your dream barn and riding arena. (If you desire a greater challenge, sketch it and label the amenities.)

Jot down 10 items on your horse bucket list. Then reflect on three horse-related activities you've done that might be on someone else's bucket list.

List the top 7 breeds of horses you would like to ride in order of preference.

_____

_____

_____

_____

_____

_____

_____

_____

_____

_____

_____

_____

Lucky you, you're heading to a horse show! What's on your packing list?

_____

_____

_____

_____

_____

_____

_____

_____

_____

_____

_____

12

From poll to dock, withers to frog—list from memory all the parts of a horse.

Delightful Descriptions

"Show, don't tell," is a phrase English teachers LOVE to use. Full disclosure: I know this because I used to be an English teacher. What teachers mean is "bring your writing alive with vivid verbs and awesome adjectives."

I learned how to show not tell my senior year of high school when my English teacher banned the use of the word "is." Yup. We would get points taken off for using the passive "am, is, are, was, were, be, being, been" verbs.

But you know what? We survived, and our writing advanced. Instead of saying, "The class was happy when they graduated and could use 'is' again," I'd say, "The seniors oozed enthusiasm upon graduation, thereby gaining the right to re-introduce 'is' into their writing."

Your turn to "show, don't tell." I won't forbid you from using "is," but if you abandon it, you might be surprised how showy your writing becomes.

What has been your most embarrassing moment around horses?

_____

_____

_____

_____

_____

_____

_____

_____

_____

_____

_____

_____

Who was the first horse you fell in love with?
Describe that horse and your relationship.

Find a favorite photograph of you with a horse. Now write about what was happening outside of the frame.

_____

_____

_____

_____

_____

_____

_____

_____

_____

_____

If you could try one new riding discipline or activity that is completely new to you, what would it be and why would you choose it?

What is the scariest fall you've ever experienced on horseback? Funniest fall? Write about one or both. (See mentor text at saddleseekshorse.com/horse-writing-prompts for my response to prompt #17).

_____

_____

_____

_____

_____

_____

_____

_____

_____

_____

What is one thing you would change about the horse industry if you could? Why is that cause important to you?

Describe an item from your riding wardrobe that you no longer wear or own, but you loved and wish you could bring back.

_____

_____

_____

_____

_____

_____

_____

_____

_____

_____

_____

Who is the best senior horse you know? What makes him or her so special? What stories do you think he or she could tell?

_____

_____

_____

_____

_____

_____

_____

_____

_____

What's the weirdest quirk you've known in a horse? What's the weirdest quirk you've known in a rider? What quirks do you possess?

_____

_____

_____

_____

_____

_____

_____

_____

_____

_____

What is your favorite quote or saying on the topic of horses? How has it inspired you?

_____

_____

_____

_____

_____

_____

_____

_____

_____

_____

_____

Got cats? Dogs? Goats? Describe the non-horsey barn critters who hang out with the horses you know.

_____

_____

_____

_____

_____

_____

_____

_____

_____

_____

Write a chronology of what you do when you go riding. Be sure to use transition words and phrases like "first," "next," or "after that" to explain the routine you follow in order to ride.

_____

_____

_____

_____

_____

_____

_____

_____

_____

_____

_____

What have been the three best horse-related times in your life?

_____

_____

_____

_____

_____

_____

_____

_____

_____

_____

_____

_____

Paint a Picture (with Words)

A picture is worth a thousand words, so they say. In this next section are several photos for you to run wild with on the page. Some of my fondest memories of writing as a kid started when a teacher would hold up a picture of something, perhaps a brooding forest or a spicy-colored parrot, and we'd get to let our imagination dream up any kind of story. How do you interpret the following horse-centric photos?

Nose to Nose

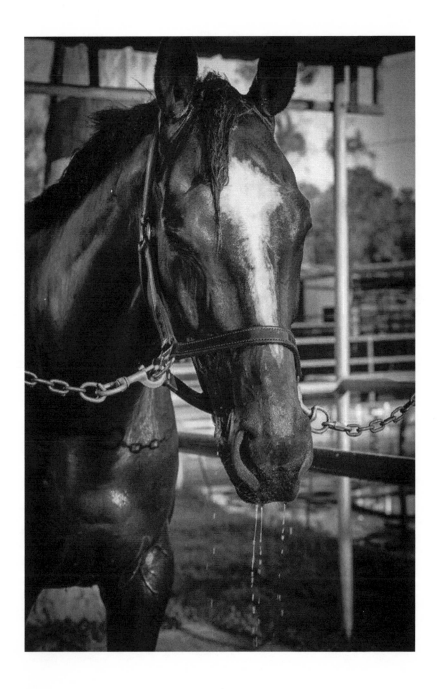

Wash Rack

Barn

_____

_____

_____

_____

_____

_____

_____

_____

_____

_____

_____

_____

_____

_____

Between the Ears

_____

_____

_____

_____

_____

_____

_____

_____

_____

_____

_____

_____

_____

_____

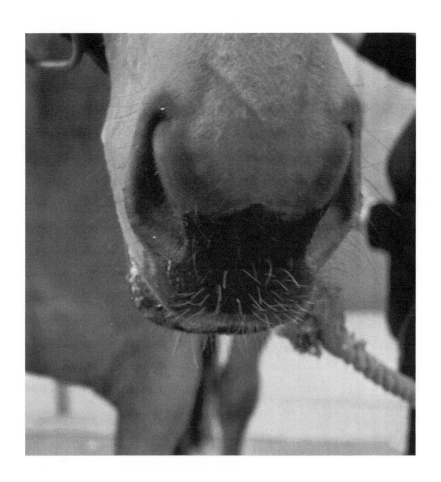

Muzzle

Boots

Saddle

_____

_____

_____

_____

_____

_____

_____

_____

_____

_____

_____

_____

_____

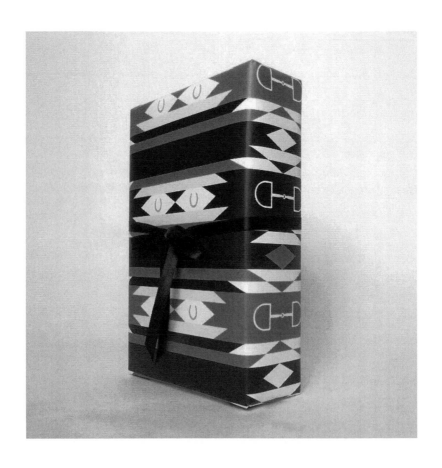

Present

Four Legs

_____

_____

_____

_____

_____

_____

_____

_____

_____

_____

_____

_____

_____

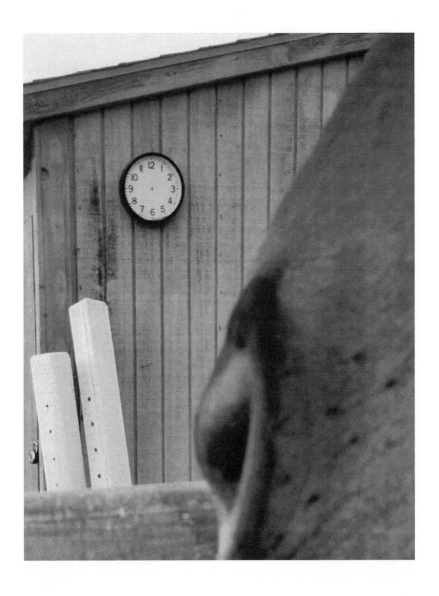

Barn Time

(Visit saddleseekshorse.com/horse-writing-prompts to see the mentor text for Barn Time.)

_____

_____

_____

_____

_____

_____

_____

_____

_____

_____

_____

Solitude

Later

_____

_____

_____

_____

_____

_____

_____

_____

_____

_____

_____

_____

_____

All About Me

Have you ever discovered yourself through writing? There have been times I was able to process a problem or clarify a goal by writing about it. I've also been able to get to know myself on a deeper level. In this next section, you'll take some time to ponder personal questions. You just might unearth some new and exciting information about yourself. Have fun!

Why do you think you love horses so much? Is it genetics? Proximity? Something else?

_____

_____

_____

_____

_____

_____

_____

_____

_____

_____

Holidays and horses. Do you have any special traditions related to any of the holidays and horses? Sleigh rides in winter? Bobbing for apples or dressing up for Halloween?

_____

_____

_____

_____

_____

_____

_____

_____

_____

What ideas do you have to make riding a more mainstream activity or hobby? How can the next generation of horsewomen and men be raised up?

_____

_____

_____

_____

_____

_____

_____

_____

_____

_____

If a Hollywood producer approached you to make a documentary about your life, what would be the title of the show, who would be the main characters, and what would be the overarching problem or conflict that drives the storyline?

_____

_____

_____

_____

_____

_____

_____

_____

Failure can be a fabulous teacher. When have you failed, and what did you learn from it?

_____

_____

_____

_____

_____

_____

_____

_____

_____

_____

_____

What emotions do horses bring out in you?

If you could meet any famous horse person living or dead and spend a day with them, shadowing their work, who would it be and what would you learn?

_____

_____

_____

_____

_____

_____

_____

_____

_____

_____

_____

45

What is the most heart-warming, true horse story you've ever heard? Jot down the details as though you were writing a synopsis for a movie script.

_____

_____

_____

_____

_____

_____

_____

_____

_____

_____

If money were no object and you could select your fanciest dreamhorse, what breed, age, color, temperament, and discipline would your horse be and do?

_____

_____

_____

_____

_____

_____

_____

_____

_____

_____

Describe five things that will get you in trouble when riding.

_____

_____

_____

_____

_____

_____

_____

_____

_____

_____

Ten years from now ...

_____

_____

_____

_____

_____

_____

_____

_____

_____

_____

_____

_____

_____

_____

What do you wish people knew about you?

What's a song you sing to your horse? If you
don't sing to your horse, what song would your
horse sing to you if he or she could?

_____

_____

_____

_____

_____

_____

_____

_____

_____

_____

Do you have a riding superstition? What is it, why do you have it, and how do you follow it?

_____

_____

_____

_____

_____

_____

_____

_____

_____

_____

_____

What is an uncomfortable truth about your passion for horses?

_____

_____

_____

_____

_____

_____

_____

_____

_____

_____

_____

_____

53

The spookiest spook I ever sat was when ... ?
The spookiest spook that landed me on the
ground was ... ?

Write about a time when you tried your best and it didn't work out the way you'd hoped it would. What happened, and how did you get over it?

_____

_____

_____

_____

_____

_____

_____

_____

_____

_____

Horses are expensive, there's no getting around it. What has been your best bargain-hunting experience? What did you get, and how did you swing such a deal?
(Visit saddleseekshorse.com/horse-writing-prompts to see the mentor text for #55.)

_____

_____

_____

_____

_____

_____

_____

_____

_____

Write about something you did in the past year that made you proud.

_____

_____

_____

_____

_____

_____

_____

_____

_____

_____

_____

_____

Pleasant Persuasion

My persuasion education all started at a young age: "Can I have a horse?" This art of persuasion is possibly one of the most practical for daily life. Whether speaking at city hall to keep a horse farm from turning into soccer fields, requesting some kind of compensation after a nightmare customer service experience, or asking for donations on behalf of wildfire victims, persuasion is important to practice. Why? Well, for one, persuasion helps you get what you want. What's not to love about that?

57

To shoe or not to shoe. Where do you stand on
the topic of horses wearing shoes or
going barefoot?

_____

_____

_____

_____

_____

_____

_____

_____

_____

_____

_____

Pegasus or a unicorn? If you had the chance to own a mythical creature, which would you choose and why?

_____

_____

_____

_____

_____

_____

_____

_____

_____

_____

Helmets or no helmets? Do you always wear a helmet when you ride? Explain your rationale for or against helmets. (Visit saddleseekshorse.com/horse-writing-prompts to see the mentor text for #59.)

_____

_____

_____

_____

_____

_____

_____

_____

_____

When you get the question, "Is riding really exercise? The horse does all the work," how do you respond?

_____

_____

_____

_____

_____

_____

_____

_____

_____

_____

If you could snap your fingers and automatically have the skills of your veterinarian or your farrier, which skill set would you choose and why?

Think of someone you know who is not that into horses. Now write a letter from the point of view of a horse you know trying to win over said person. (If you like a greater challenge, actually give the letter to him or her.)

What aspect of grooming a horse do you like the least and why? What aspect of grooming a horse is your favorite and why?

_____

_____

_____

_____

_____

_____

_____

_____

_____

_____

_____

Chestnuts mares: evil or elegant? What's your opinion of the redheaded ladies?

_____

_____

_____

_____

_____

_____

_____

_____

_____

_____

_____

Spirit, Black Beauty or Seabiscuit: Which horse would you choose to ride and why?

_____

_____

_____

_____

_____

_____

_____

_____

_____

_____

_____

_____

Horses are better than humans. Do you agree?
What arguments would you choose to back up
your stance on this statement?

_____

_____

_____

_____

_____

_____

_____

_____

_____

_____

Do you think it's wiser to buy an inexpensive green horse you can train for your particular discipline, or to purchase a more expensive horse that already has the experience and training? Explain your viewpoint.

_____

_____

_____

_____

_____

_____

_____

_____

_____

_____

Deep and Thoughtful

From imagined conversations with acquaintances from days of yore to pondering current ethical dilemmas, this section will require you to think on a deep level and come up with innovative ideas. This section is best used when you have a little extra time to contemplate while you write.

68

You track down the first riding instructor you
ever had; write your conversation.

_____

_____

_____

_____

_____

_____

_____

_____

_____

_____

_____

If there were a barn fire, besides your horse and tack (assume they made it out safely), what would you run out of the barn area carrying in your arms?

_____

_____

_____

_____

_____

_____

_____

_____

_____

_____

Everyone has at least one special talent or gift. What's one of yours?

_____

_____

_____

_____

_____

_____

_____

_____

_____

_____

_____

_____

71

Describe your worst experience horse shopping (and if you have never had a bad horse shopping experience, your worst dating experience).

_____

_____

_____

_____

_____

_____

_____

_____

_____

_____

_____

Chronicle an ethical dilemma you've faced in the horse world.

_____

_____

_____

_____

_____

_____

_____

_____

_____

_____

_____

73

Why do you like your current riding boots?

_____

_____

_____

_____

_____

_____

_____

_____

_____

_____

_____

_____

_____

What is your biggest fear related to horses? How do you manage this fear?

_____

_____

_____

_____

_____

_____

_____

_____

_____

_____

_____

_____

A conversation you weren't supposed to hear at the barn was ...

What horse magazine doesn't exist that you think should?

_____

_____

_____

_____

_____

_____

_____

_____

_____

_____

_____

_____

What are your favorite money-saving tips for your horse passion?

_____

_____

_____

_____

_____

_____

_____

_____

_____

_____

_____

What do you think are the most common misconceptions non horse people have about horse people?

_____

_____

_____

_____

_____

_____

_____

_____

_____

_____

79

If there was one horse-related invention that you could bring to the world—even if you don't have the technical expertise or budget to do so— what would it be? (Visit saddleseekshorse.com/horse-writing-prompts to see the mentor text for #79.)

What is the most unorthodox riding outfit you've observed someone pull off?

_____

_____

_____

_____

_____

_____

_____

_____

_____

_____

_____

You are alone on a desert island with only your horse. What five necessities would you need for the two of you to survive?

Creative and Cool

If I had to pick a favorite section, this would be the one (don't tell the other sections!). If doodling and poetry are fun for you, this might be your favorite section too. I mean, what's not to love about a limerick? In addition, if you enjoy humor and express yourself that way, this is the section to make yourself smirk while writing.

If you were a horse, what kind of horse would you be? Explain by telling a story using vivid verbs and sensory images.

_____

_____

_____

_____

_____

_____

_____

_____

_____

_____

_____

Write a sales ad your horse would create to sell you. Don't forget to list the asking price and give contact information. If you want to be really ethical, be sure to include vices.

_____

_____

_____

_____

_____

_____

_____

_____

_____

_____

_____

_____

Do You haiku? Short and sweet with no rhymes, employing the 5 syllable, 7 syllable, 5 syllable format, these Japanese poems were initially meant to celebrate nature. You're going to write a haiku (or two) to celebrate a horse.

Limerick. No St. Patrick's Day in elementary school would have been complete without writing limericks. The five-line poem with lines 1, 2 and 5 possessing the same rhyme and lines 3 and 4 matching with a different rhyme is meant to be silly, sarcastic or nonsensical. If you need a sample to get started, think back to this old nursery rhyme:

Hickory, dickory, dock
The mouse ran up the clock
The clock struck one
The mouse ran down
Hickory dickory dock

Interview your horse: Write a Q&A column like those where celebrities are questioned on their careers or their favorite things (like books, vacation spots, clothing items, et cetera). Your horse is the celebrity, and you get to dive deep into your most pressing questions.

Acrostic: Did you ever have to write an acrostic with your first name in elementary school? This time around, you're going to write an acrostic with the name of a horse. If your horse has a really short name (like my heart horse, DC), use their show name, registered name or perhaps the name of a different horse you know who has a longer name.

Recipe: Remember that saying "sugar and spice and everything nice"? That's supposedly what little girls are made of. Now's your chance to get culinary and write a recipe telling what your horse is made of. One bale of alfalfa plus a pound of apples mixed in with 4 cups of sweetness, a heaping tablespoon of lazy, and a pinch of jigging on trail could be the basis for my horse. What is your horse made of?

_____

_____

_____

_____

_____

_____

_____

I Am Poem: This type of poem doesn't typically rhyme. It's actually simple in essence—you will just complete the statements to describe yourself.

I am _____

I wonder _____

I hear _____

I see _____

I pretend _____

I feel _____

I touch _____

I worry _____

I cry _____

I understand _____

I say _____

I dream _____

I try _____

I hope _____

A to Z: An A to Z poem is kind of like an acrostic, but the starting letter for each line of poetry will go in alphabetical order. When finished, you will have a 26-line poem celebrating your horse, riding, or any equestrian theme.

Low-tech "Polaroid": On this page, draw a few pictures of your horse, you and your horse together, or something horse-related, like your boots. Write captions for each. If you really want to go all out, grab your colored pencils or markers and add dazzling color.

_____

_____

_____

_____

_____

_____

_____

_____

_____

_____

_____

Using words and pictures (stick figures are fine), create a comic strip of you and your horse together. Suggested comics could be a time you fell, tried to catch your horse, or any other episode that has a humorous twist.

_____

_____

_____

_____

_____

_____

_____

_____

_____

93

Write a review of your last ride from the point of view of the horse you rode. How many stars would you receive?

_____

_____

_____

_____

_____

_____

_____

_____

_____

_____

_____

Song parody: Channel your inner Weird Al Yankovic. Think of a catchy tune and swap out the lyrics to be a song about the horse you love. Instead of Sonny and Cher's "I Got You Babe," write lyrics to "I Rode You, Bay." Or instead of changing the title of a song, just insert new, horsey lyrics into an existing one. For example, Taylor Swift's "You Need to Calm Down" might apply to your horse. Have fun and get creative.

_____

_____

_____

_____

_____

_____

_____

_____

Fast Fiction

Writing stories for fun stimulates the imagination, but unfortunately, it seems the older we get, the more we are forced into writing non-fiction. Emails, texts, presentations and research papers dwell in the realm of the practical and real. But some of the most entertaining words to string together are those that weave a narrative born straight from inspiration—characters and adventures invented just for entertainment. Enjoy this last section and turn your mind out to pasture to buck and gallop free.

95

Due to unforeseen events, you end up staying late at the barn. It's midnight, and there's a full moon. Your horse starts to speak, thinking you're out of earshot. What happens next?

A hoof pick, a vintage horse show trophy and a magical tack trunk: Write a short story or scene based on these three elements.

You have a Breyer horse collection in your bedroom or office. You go on vacation for two weeks, and upon your return, the model horses are scattered throughout your house, all looking out windows. Write a few creative paragraphs that explain what happened.

_____

_____

_____

_____

_____

_____

_____

_____

You are summoned to be a special riding guest of Queen Elizabeth II. What will you wear, and what would you want to talk to her about? Draft a dialogue you think might actually take place between you and Her Royal Highness.

_____

_____

_____

_____

_____

_____

_____

_____

_____

_____

Everyone loves an underdog story. Create characters for your own horse underdog story, and either write a scene or synopsis.

_____

_____

_____

_____

_____

_____

_____

_____

_____

_____

Thanks to innovations in technology, time travel becomes a reality. Where and when will you travel in order to check out the horses?

_____

_____

_____

_____

_____

_____

_____

_____

_____

_____

What is your horse story? Who do you think needs to hear it, and where can you share it? (I would love to read it! Tag me on social media @saddleseekshorse.)

_____

_____

_____

_____

_____

_____

_____

_____

_____

_____

Notes

Author's Note and Contact Info

I hope you are having a blast writing about horses. If you would like to connect, here's where you can find me.

- Email: susan@saddleseekshorse.com
- My email newsletter to stay in the loop: saddleseekshorse.com/sign-up
- On the blog Saddle Seeks Horse: www.saddleseekshorse.com
- Saddle Seeks Horse Facebook Page: www.facebook.com/SaddleSeeksHorse
- Instagram: www.instagram.com/saddleseekshorse
- Pinterest: www.pinterest.com/saddlseekshorse

If you enjoyed *Unbridled Creativity: 101 Writing Exercises for the Horse Lover*, it would mean so much to me if you would leave a review on Amazon or Goodreads. Reviews are gold for authors like me, as they allow more exposure to new readers. And word-of-mouth recommendations are wonderful too. Thanks for being so kind!

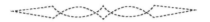
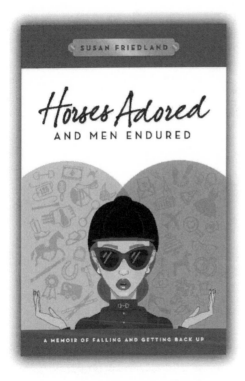

Strands of Hope
How to grieve the loss of a horse

Through personal stories, interviews and practical tips, find strands of hope for the bereaved equestrian.

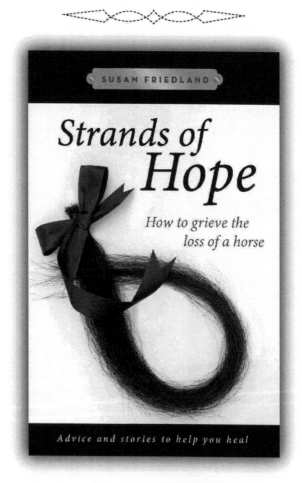

Let's Stay Connected!

You're invited to stay in the horsey loop with me.

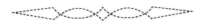

Trot along on the blog where I
share equestrian information and
inspiration for horse lovers like us.
Visit the link below to subscribe.

saddleseekshorse.com/sign-up

Tally ho - Susan